MW00461592

A Little Hug

for:

....

from:

....

date:

....

a little book of

hugs™

for
teachers

Inspiration for the Heart

**Andrews McMeel
Publishing**

Kansas City

ISBN: 0-7407-1185-7

Library of Congress Catalog Card Number: 00-102161

Messages by Caron Loveless
Personalized Scriptures by LeAnn Weiss
Interior design and illustrations by Vanessa Bearden
Project Editor: Philis Boultinghouse

CONTENTS

drawing by Annabeth, age 6

"My favorite teacher is Mrs. Calloway. She is sooo nice! She has poofy hair and wasn't like a teacher. She was like an ordinary person. She was funny, loving, caring, and always had something nice to say."

—Erin, age 10

chapter one

A Teacher Is...

100 sheets • 200 pages
9¾ x 7½ in/24.7 x 19.0 cm
wide ruled • 09910

I make you stand firm in Christ. I have anointed you, set My seal of ownership on you, and put My Spirit in your heart as a deposit, guaranteeing what is to come. I love to do far beyond all you ask or dream through My power, which is working in you—even when you don't realize it.

Love,
Your God of Victory

—2 Corinthians 1:21-22;
Ephesians 3:20

*Y*ou're a banker and an artist.
You're a sprinter and a florist.
You're an actor. You're a juggler.
You're a queen.

4

$\mathcal{Y}$ou're a lawyer.
You're a manager.
You're a nurse,
and you're a counselor.
You do more by noon
than most have ever seen.

You're a driver and a poet.
A politician (don't you know it!)
You're a botanist, a strategist,
and a judge.

You're a mother and a father.
You're a runner
and a tightrope walker.
You're a soldier fighting
in the war on drugs.

*Y*ou're a diplomat
and an acrobat.
You're a farmer.
You're a friend.
You tell stories.
You mend fences.
You build dreams.

You're an instructor
and a trainer,
a communicator
and demonstrator.
You're a teacher!
You're incredible!
You're supreme!

Essentially, learning
means a change in your
thinking, a change in your
feeling, a change in your
behavior. Learning means
that change takes place in
the mind, in the emotions,
and in the will.
—Howard G. Hendricks

②

chapter two

A Teacher's Gifts

100 sheets • 200 pages
9¾ x 7½ in/24.7 x 19.0 cm
wide ruled • 09910

I've started a good work in you. When you feel overwhelmed and at the end of your rope, look up and remember that your help comes from Me! Please don't lose heart in doing good, for in My perfect timing I promise you'll see a reward if you don't give up. Be confident that I will faithfully complete the things I've birthed in you.

Love,
Your God of Redemption

—Psalm 121:1–2;
Galatians 6:9; Philippians 1:6

$\mathcal{I}$t doesn't stop here, you know. Like dandelion seeds strewn across a meadow, what you do just keeps on going.

God takes your acts of love, those wispy, wiry pods, and launches them out with the gust of His breath. The deeds of your hands are sprinkled here and there throughout the land, escorted by the winds of His Spirit. No. It doesn't stop here. It multiplies.

$\mathcal{L}$ike rippling rings on a pond, your encouraging words, your positive reinforcements, and your assuring smiles are all going places. Places that thirst for these things, places you could never go yourself, into lives you'll never get to meet.

$\mathcal{B}$ut really, you want it this way. It's the way it was for you. You yourself are a ring from someone else's splashing rock. Like branches of shade, your effort doesn't stop here. It goes on to cool other souls. Like you, it will reach out, comfort, shelter, and accept.

*N*one of it stops with you. It started with you, but it won't stop there. Not by a long shot.

Your students will carry your gifts away. Your kind words, your pure passions, and your guiding light will be passed out by them like bread to the hungry.

They will take your humble light and set off diamonds in the sky. There will be fireworks in the future. People will gasp at their dazzling display, delight in their shimmering brilliance—all ablaze from your one tiny spark.

Oh no, dear teacher.
It doesn't stop here.

A teacher affects
eternity;
he can never tell
where his
influence stops.

—Henry Adams

❸

chapter three

A Teacher's Worth

100 sheets • 200 pages
9¾ x 7½ in/24.7 x 19.0 cm
wide ruled • 09910

The fear of My Father is the beginning of wisdom, and knowledge of the Holy One is understanding. Hold to My teaching and you will know the truth. My truth will set you free.

Love,
Jesus

—Proverbs 9:10;
John 8:31–32

Much of your life has been focused on grades. First, there were grades you had to make to please your parents. Then came grades you had to get to enter college. And now, it's grades that you must give to all your students.

*I*n fact, grades have probably become such a priority that if you were asked the question, "If your house were on fire and you could take out only one book…" no doubt you'd say, "My grade book!"

$\mathcal{G}$rades are helpful—they're important measuring tools. Grades are motivating—they often spur achievers on to greatness. But after being in an atmosphere of evaluation for a long time, you might begin to compare yourself to others— and that can spell trouble.

*S*ome things just weren't
designed to be graded....

Can you grade a glowing sunset
or flashing bugs inside a jar?
Can you rate a velvet rose
or score the sparkle of a star?

*D*are you judge
between a dewdrop
and the swells that
storm at sea?
Can you gauge a gliding swan
or appraise the sweetness
of a peach?

What's the measure of a
mountain?
What's the rank of rabbit's skin?
What's the status of a fountain?
Try to grade a baby's grin.

When you were born, God didn't give you a grade; rather, He announced His opinion of you to the whole world. And it was…very good!

The whole art of teaching is only the art of awakening the natural curiosity of young minds for the purpose of satisfying it afterwards.

—Anatole France

Every good teacher is a student of students. After all, if he is to venture to cross over to the student's side of experience, he should have some idea of where he is going, and how to get there.

—Wayne R. Rood

4

chapter four

A Teacher's Legacy

100 sheets • 200 pages
9¾ x 7½ in/24.7 x 19.0 cm
wide ruled • 09910

43

I am for you! Watch Me multiply your efforts. Because of My power working in you, the outcome is far beyond all that you can ask or dream. Nothing is too difficult for Me.

Faithfully,
Your God of Victory

—Romans 8:31;
Ephesians 3:20; Jeremiah 32:17

*A*mong all your former teachers, who is the one that to this day inspires you? Who first challenged you to "think outside the box"?

Who took special interest in your work? Who motivated you to get to class early, stay up late, or dream bigger dreams?

*W*hich one of your teachers
or professors awakened you to
a subject that had a previous
history of putting you to sleep?

Which teacher stoked your courage to give a speech, try out for a play, or apply for a coveted scholarship? Of all of them, who was it you lived to please most?

Why not stop for a moment and visit that teacher again? Recall the wonder you felt in her presence. Think about the new direction you pursued as a result of his comments or her advice. Imagine what you would have missed had that teacher not been assigned to you.

$\mathcal{B}$elieve it or not, this week some student is looking up at you with the same sense of awe you felt for your teacher. Somewhere amidst the sea of often blank faces, a student is leaning in to catch your every word. He is listening. She is getting it. Thanks to you.

*L*et the honor sink in. Let the thought of it invigorate your lessons. Celebrate the fact that long after you're gone, your name and today's investment will be alive and thriving in someone's soul.

One day, you may see these students again, hear of their achievements, and feel it was worth all the effort. Until then, bask in the knowledge that every time you teach, you invest in your own living legacy.

In teaching you cannot see the fruit of a day's work. It is invisible and remains so, maybe for twenty years.

—Jacques Barzun

chapter five

A Teacher's Thanks

100 sheets • 200 pages
9¾ x 7½ in/24.7 x 19.0 cm
wide ruled • 09910

Teacher, may the Lord repay you for what you have done. May you be richly rewarded by the Lord, under whose wings you have come to take refuge. Delight yourself in the Lord, and He will fulfill your heart's desires. Commit your ways to Him and trust Him, and He will do it. He'll help you shine!

Love,
Your God of
Encouragement

—Ephesians 6:8;
Psalms 16:1; 91:4; 37:4–6

$\mathcal{D}$ear Teacher,

Thank you for taking the time to talk to me in the hall the other day. You didn't know it, but what you said came at just the right time. I ended up not doing something that I now know would have been really stupid.

Thanks for the note you wrote in the margin of my paper fifteen years ago. I doubt you remember it, but I sure do. It stirred something in me. It lit a fuse that hasn't stopped burning. I'm a writer now. I hope that makes you proud. Enclosed is a copy of my first book.

Thanks for really being interested in the point I was trying to make in class last week. I think it's the first time a teacher has ever taken me seriously. It felt good.

Thanks for the personal challenge. I needed it.

Thanks for making school fun. The way you explain things, I don't even mind taking notes.

$\mathcal{T}$hanks for showing up every day. You're the only one in my life who does.

$\mathcal{T}$hanks for knowing my name.

Thanks for believing in me
even when everybody else
(including me) predicted failure.
I don't know what you saw in
me. You put up with a lot.
Thanks for not giving up.

$\mathcal{O}$h, and thanks for all the homework (just kidding!).
Love,
Your Students

Education is not to reform students or amuse them or to make them expert technicians. It is to unsettle their minds, widen their horizons, inflame their intellect, teach them to think straight, if possible.

—Robert M. Hutchins

drawing by Alisa, age 9

"Mrs. Bennett was the bestest teacher I had. She was fun, sweet, and nice. I once gave her some chocalate and she ate it."

—Ginnie, age 8

Look for these other little *Hugs* books:

A Little Book of Hugs for Friends
A Little Book of Hugs for Mom
A Little Book of Hugs for Women
A Little Book of Hugs for Sisters
A Little Book of Hugs to Encourage and Inspire

Also look for these full-size *Hugs* books:

Hugs for Women
Hugs for Friends
Hugs for Mom
Hugs for Kids
Hugs for Teachers
Hugs for Sisters
Hugs for Those in Love
Hugs for the Hurting
Hugs for Grandparents
Hugs for Dad
Hugs for the Holidays
Hugs to Encourage and Inspire